SOUTH AFRICA
by PIKTUREBOX

photography by benjamin garret ryder

BABEL

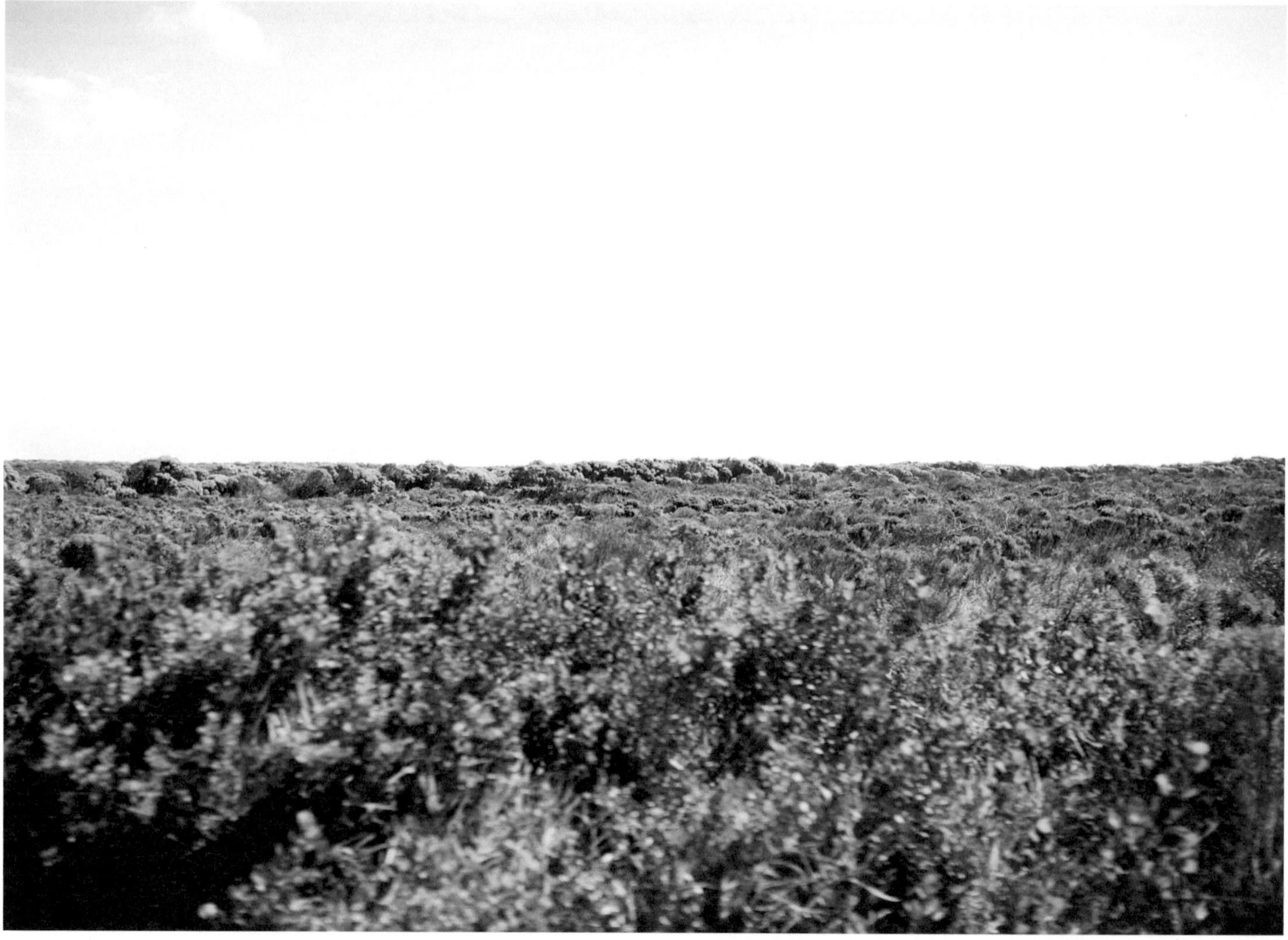

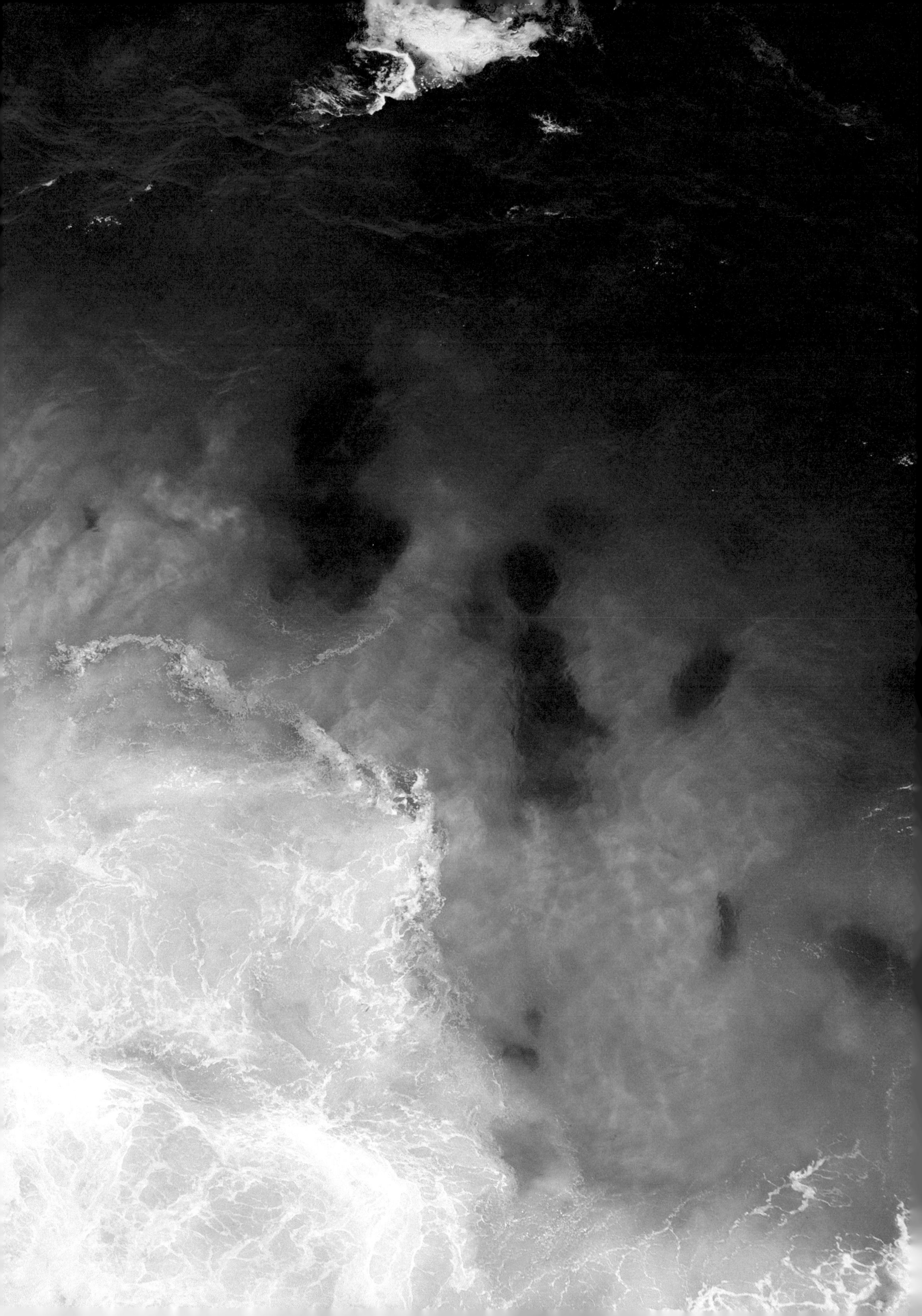

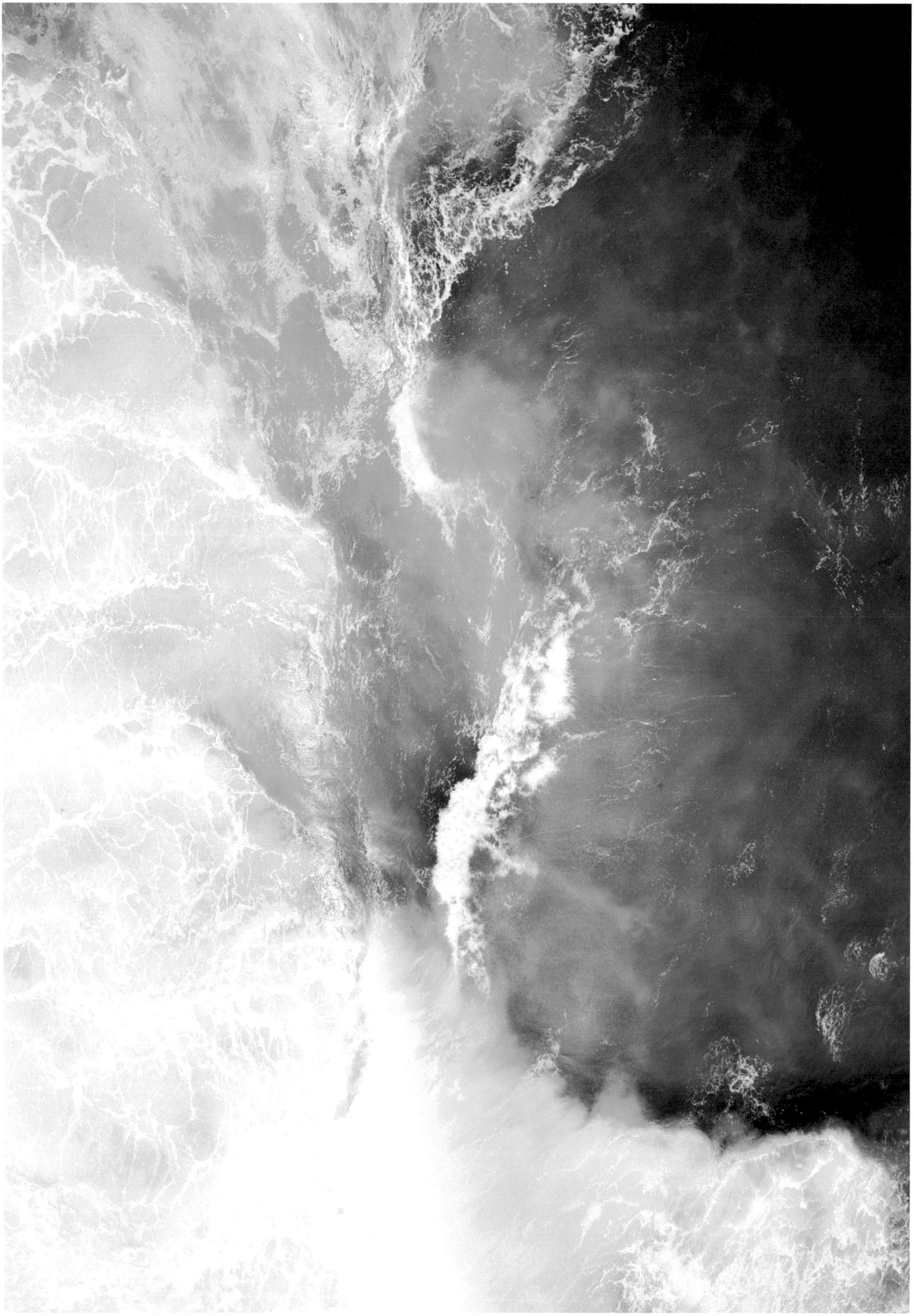

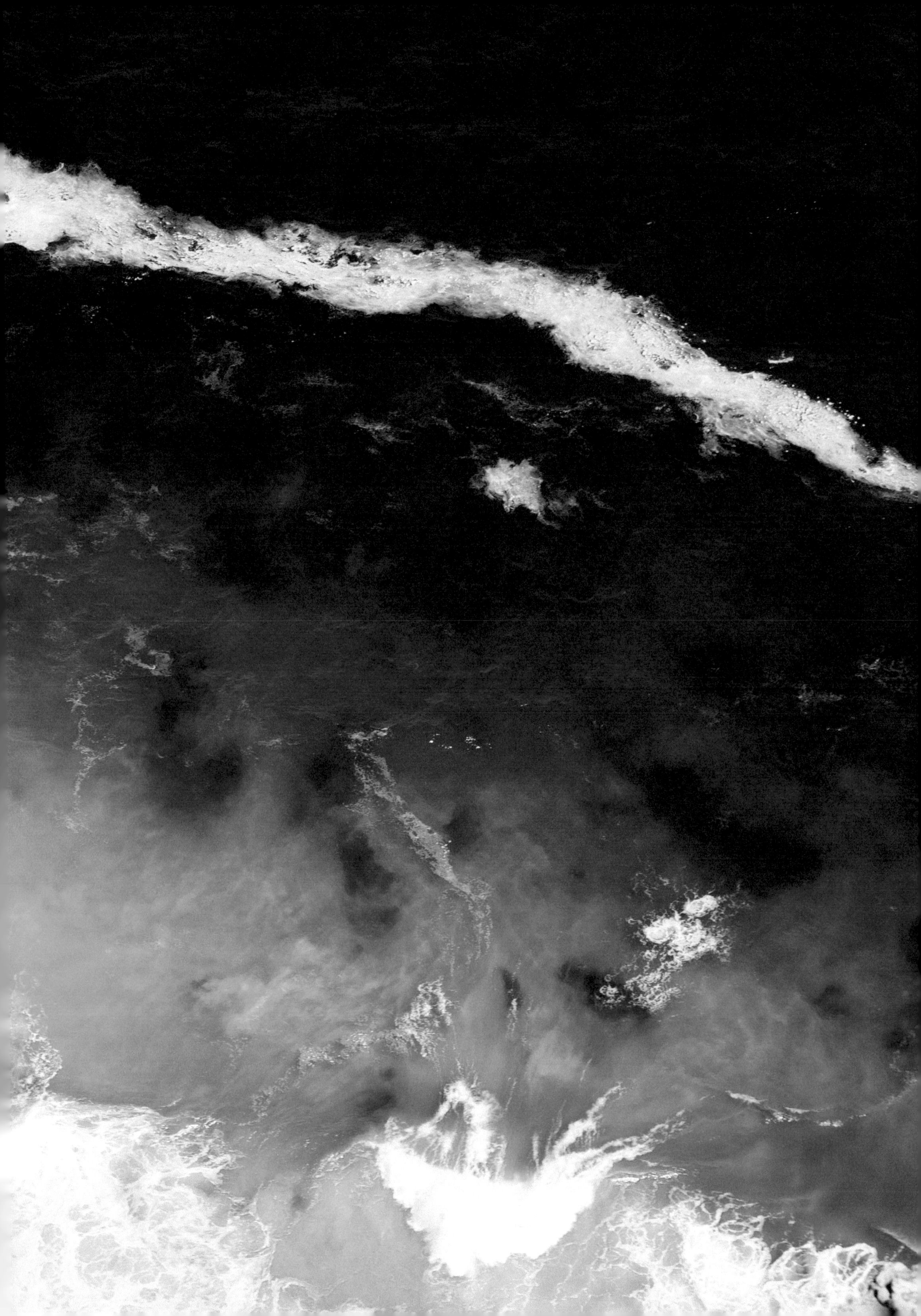

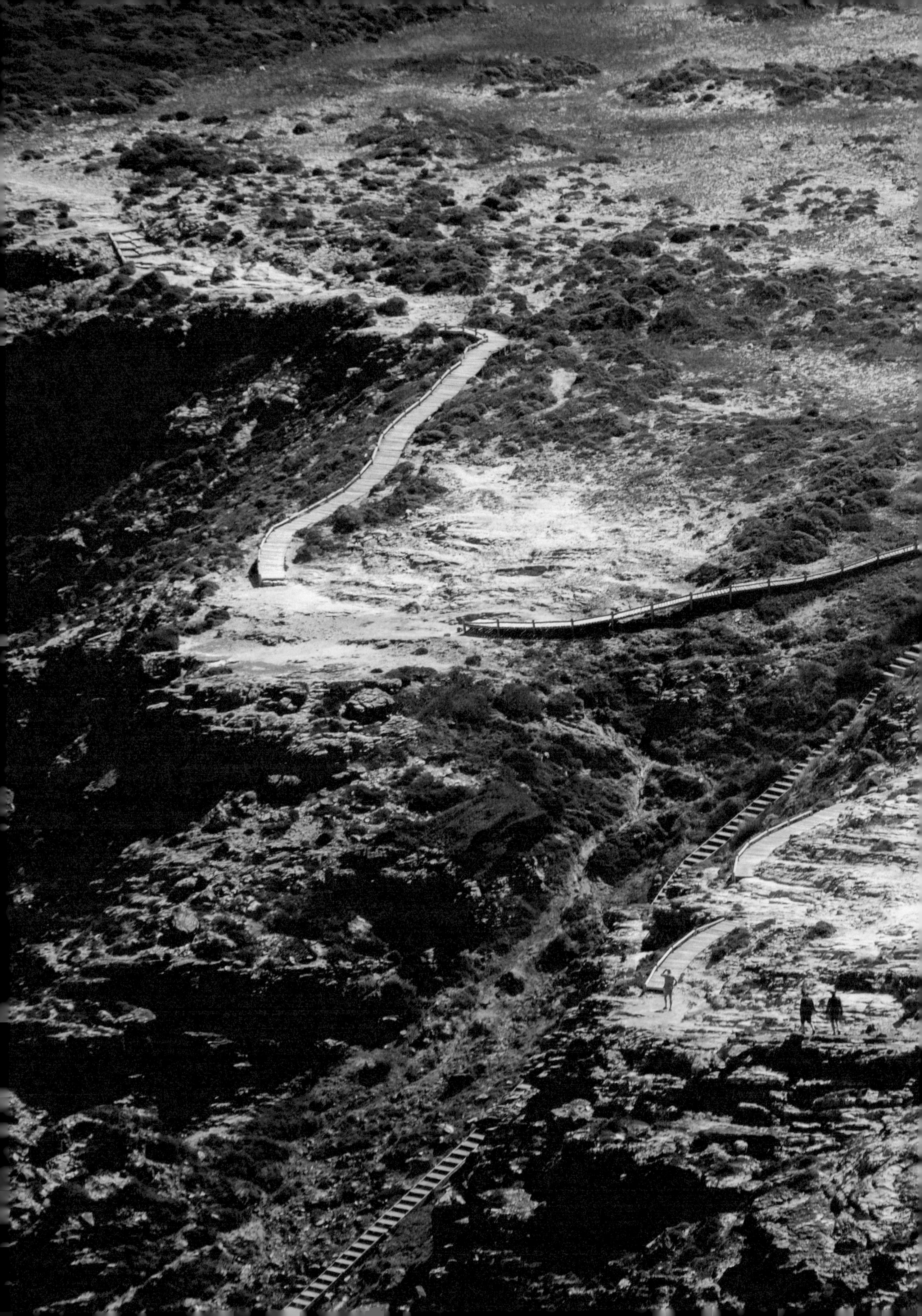

60
CHILDREN
KINDERS

Made in the USA
Columbia, SC
13 December 2024

7440e5fc-338c-43ea-9c93-df23991005e7R01